# My
# Thanksgiving

Jennifer Blizin Gillis

Raintree

Chicago, Illinois

Customer Service  888-363-4266
Visit our website at www.raintreelibrary.com

Designed by Joanna Hinton-Malivoire and Tokay
Printed and bound in China by South China Printing Company

10 09 08 07 06
10 9 8 7 6 5 4 3 2 1

Library of Congress Cataloging-in-Publication Data
Gillis, Jennifer Blizin, 1950-
  My Thanksgiving / Jennifer Blizin Gillis.
      p. cm. --  (Festivals)
  Includes bibliographical references and index.
  ISBN 1-4109-1403-8 (pb) -- ISBN 1-4109-1402-X (hc)
  1.  Thanksgiving Day--Juvenile literature.  I. Title. II. Series: Festivals
(Raintree Publishers)
  GT4975.G55 2005
  394.2649--dc22

                          2004023083

Acknowledgments
The author and publisher are grateful to the following for permission to reproduce copyright material:
Corbis pp.6 (Bettmann), 16 (Tom Stewart), 20 (Jose Luis Pelaez, Inc.); Getty Images pp.4 (Digital
Vision), 5 (Photodisc Green/Spike Mafford), 8 (Stone/Eric Larrayadieu), 12 (Photodisc Green), 19 (The
Image Bank/David W. Hamilton); Harcourt Index/Photodisc Green/Ryan McVay pp.14; Photo Edit, Inc.
pp.7 (Felicia Martinez), 10 (Myrleen Ferguson Cate), 11 (Bill Bachmann), 13 (David Young-Wolff), 15
(Michelle D. Bridwell), 17 (Richard Hutchings), 18 (Jose Carillo); PictureQuest pp.21 (Photodisc), 22
(Creatas); Richard Levine pp.9.

Cover photograph reproduced with permission of Corbis/Paul Barton.

Every effort has been made to contact copyright holders of any material reproduced in this book.
Any omissions will be rectified in subsequent printings if notice is given to the publisher.

Some words are shown in bold, **like this**. You can find out
what they mean by looking in the glossary on page 24.

# Contents

# Thanksgiving Time

It is November.
It is **fall**.

Thanksgiving is in November.
It is always on Thursday.

# Thanksgiving at School

Native Americans

Pilgrims

We learn about the
first Thanksgiving.

We dress up like pilgrims.

7

# Shopping

We go to the store.
We help with the shopping.

We buy a turkey. It is big!

# Helping Others

Feed the Hungry

Donate Food

Thanksgiving is a time to share.

We share our food.

We help our neighbors.

# Thanksgiving Decorations

We help mom fill a **horn of plenty**.

We make turkey decorations.

# Special Treats

We make pumpkin pie.

Yummy!

We make rolls. I help **sift** the flour.

15

Getting Ready

Vroom!

We clean the house.

16

17

# Thanksgiving Day

We cook the turkey.

We watch a parade on television.

# Family and Friends

Grandma and grandpa are here.

20

Our aunt, uncle, and cousins are here, too. We will spend Thanksgiving together.

21

# A Special Meal

We are thankful for our family.
We are thankful for our friends.

# Glossary

**fall** one of four seasons in a year. Fall months are September, October, and November.

**horn of plenty** horn-shaped basket filled with fall vegetables, such as squash and small pumpkins

**Native Americans** people who lived in America before the pilgrims came

**Pilgrims** people who came from England to live in America in the 1600s

**sift** make a powder smoother by shaking it through a screen

# Index